Hear-Say™
GERMAN

by

Donald S. Rivera

Produced and distributed by
Smart Kids™
A division of
Penton Overseas, Inc.
2470 Impala Drive, Carlsbad, CA 92008
www.pentonoverseas.com

Producer
Ron Berry

Illustrator
Chris Sharp

Sound Effects
Sunset Sounds Studio
Ron Spenser – Engineer

Exxel Audio Productions
T.W. Shelton – Recording Engineer
Rick Harchol – Mixing Engineer

Art/Editorial Director
Annette Norris

Design/Layout
Matt Shaw

German translation
Natali Davison
Astrid Ronke

German narration
Astrid Ronke

INSTRUCTIONS & CONTENTS

This entertaining **Audio Program** and fun-filled **Activity Book** will have kids of all ages speaking German in no time. For starters, it's a scientific fact…children learn a foreign language faster and more easily than adults. Now, with this exciting, new format, that combines sound effects with their German word, kids learn a foreign language naturally – just like they learn English. The audio along with the colorful, illustrated **Hear-Say Activity Book** offers a dynamic multi-sensory, interactive, language learning experience.

1. The Audio Program:

Sound Effects
Over 200 common sound effects are presented in distinct categories to facilitate recognition.

German Pronunciation
First the sound effect is heard, followed by the German word spoken twice by a native speaker. This allows the listener to learn correct pronunciation and to say the word along with the speaker.

2. The Activity Book

Visual Reinforcement
The book contains 15 colorfully illustrated scenes along with additional images that match each sound effect/word spoken on the audio. Each individual image is accompanied by the written word in German. The combination of the sound effect, the spoken pronunciation of the word, a visual image of the word and the actual written word, to develop reading skills in German presents a fully integrated, multi-sensory learning experience!

Find the Matching Picture
In addition, each action-filled environment contains a second image of the sound effect/word providing an independent activity for children to find the matching picture in its natural surroundings.

Find The Hidden Mouse
Hidden in every scene is a clever little mouse. As kids search the scene to match the word picture, they must also keep a sharp lookout to Find The Hidden Mouse!

DiE TiERE

der Hund

die Katze

der Vogel

der Hahn

die Kuh

die Ente

das Pferd

das Schwein

1

das Schaf

der Elefant

der Löwe

der Affe

der Seehund

der Frosch

der Esel

2

DIE FAHRZEUGE

das Motorrad

das Fahrrad

das Rollbrett

das Auto

der Bus

der Krankenwagen

der Zug

das Boot

das Flugzeug

der Hubschrauber

der Traktor

das Müllauto

das Feuerwehrauto

das U-Boot

4

iM HAUS

die Türklingel

die Tür

der Fernseher

das Radio

die Klimaanlage

das Telefon

der Staubsauger

der Ventilator

der Besen

5

iM BADEZiMMER

die Toilette

die Dusche

die Badewanne

die Zahnbürste

der Fön

der Rasierapparat

IN DER KÜCHE

das Geschirr

die Gläser

der Topf

der Mixer

der Dosenöffner

der Toaster

das Wasser

die Teekanne

die Limonade

das Popcorn

der Apfel

die Suppe

die Milch

das Ei

der Schinken

das Müsli

die Kartoffelchips

8

iM GARTEN

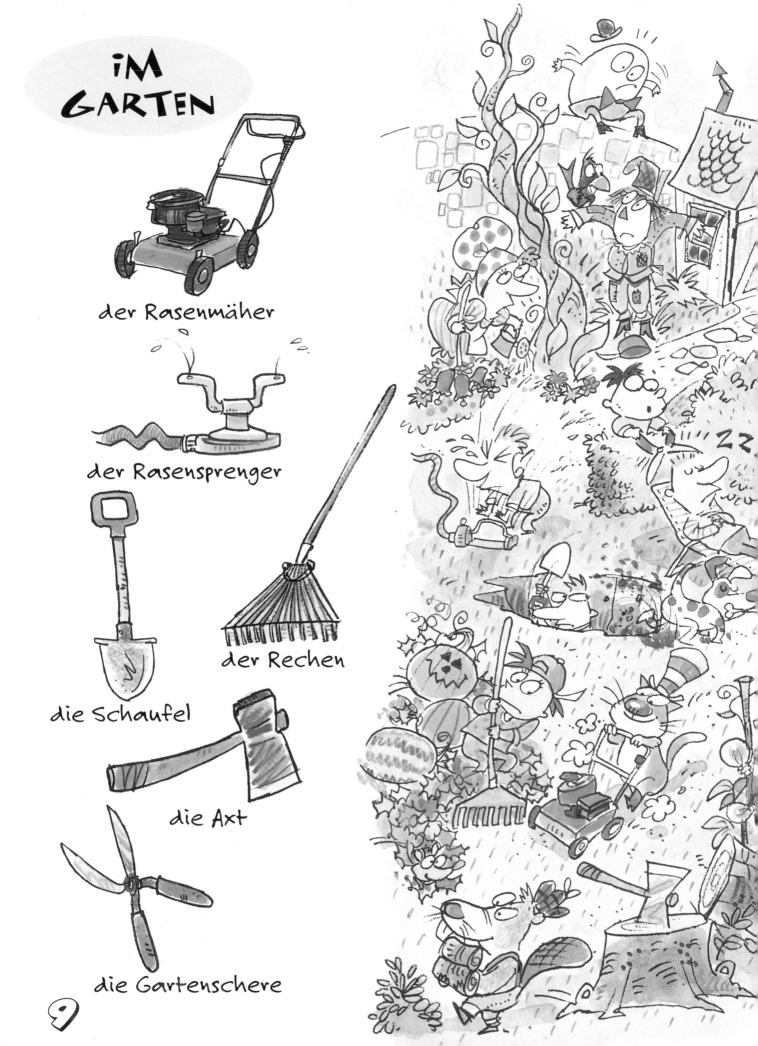

der Rasenmäher

der Rasensprenger

die Schaufel

der Rechen

die Axt

die Gartenschere

iN DER GARAGE

der Hammer

die Bohrmaschine

die Säge

das Metermass

die Nägel

der Schraubenschlüssel

der Werkzeugkasten

die Luftpumpe

die Leiter

10

PLÄTZE

die Schule

die Stadt

der Zoo

der Strand

das Büro

der Supermarkt

das Restaurant

11

das Schwimmbecken

die Turnhalle

die Tankstelle

die Kirche

das Krankenhaus

der Bauernhof

der Freizeitpark

12

MUSIK-INSTRUMENTE

die Trommel

die Trompete

die Gitarre

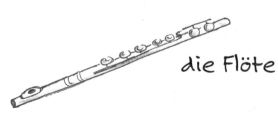
die Flöte

das Klavier

die Posaune

die Geige

die Mundharmonica

die Tuba

die Harfe

das Saxaphon

das Becken

der Bass

14

DER SPORT

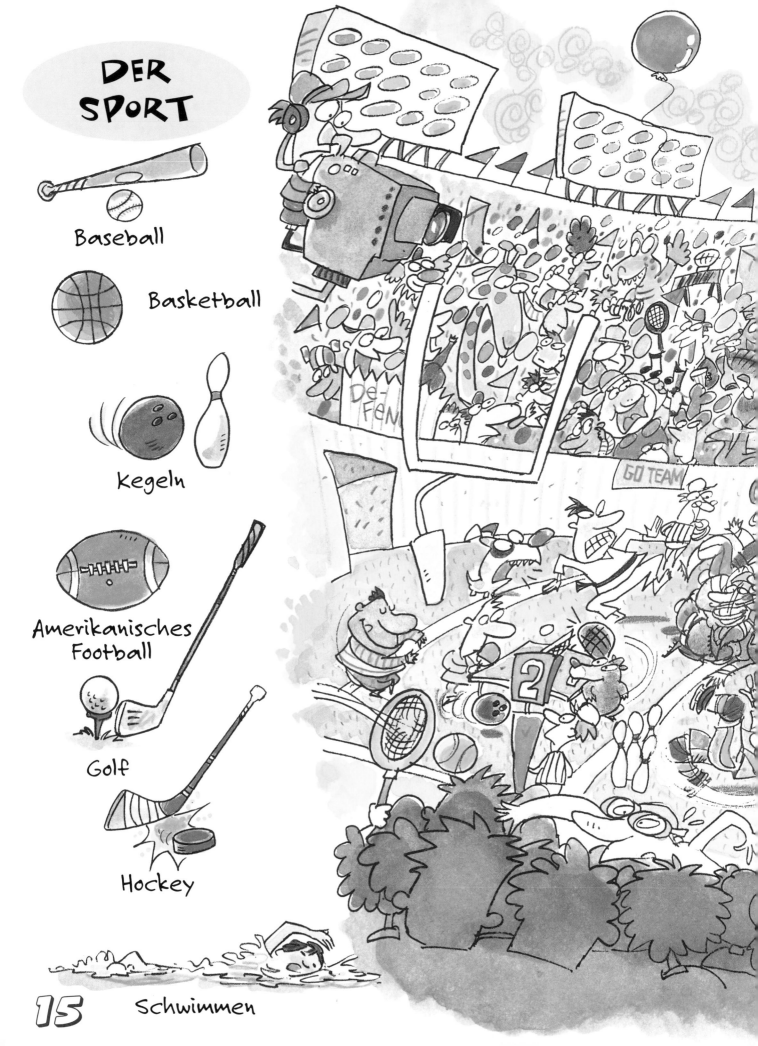

Baseball

Basketball

Kegeln

Amerikanisches Football

Golf

Hockey

Schwimmen

Tennis

Ping pong

Karate

Gewichtheben

Boxen

TÄTIG-KEITEN

laufen

rennen

essen

trinken

reden

arbeiten

spielen

schreiben

lesen

kochen

tanzen

singen

klatschen

18

KÖRPER-GERÄUSCHE

atmen

lachen

küssen

weinen

schreien

niesen

husten

19

gähnen

gurgeln

rülpsen

schnarchen

Nase schnauben

schluckauf

stöhnen

Herz schlagen

20

DiNGE

die Schlüssel

die Kamera

die Uhr

das Geld

die Pfeife

die Tasche

das Kaugummi

21

die Karten

das Buch

der Anspitzer

der Reissverschluss

das Spielzeug

die Mücke

die Fliegenklappe

MEHR DINGE

der Computer

der Roboter

das Baby

das Eis

der Ballon

der Eimer

die Flagge

JAIL

23

das Gefängnis

das Dynamit

das Papier

das Fenster

die Schere

die Schuhe

24

der Wind

DIE NATUR

der Regen

der Donner

das Feuer

der Ozean

der Wasserfall

der Dschungel

der Sumpf

der Bach

das Erdbeben

der Vulkan

die Schlucht

26

NUMMERN

Zähle die Töne!

eins

zwei

drei

vier

fünf

sechs

sieben

acht

neun

zehn

das Ende

27

Coo Coo

Coo Coos R-U

BUS STOP

28

Discover more ways to make language learning fun–

Hear-Say™
This exciting way to learn a language
is available in
English • French • German • Italian • Spanish

Word Play
Interactive Book & Audio CD
Spanish / Inglés

Lyric Language®
A Bilingual Music Program
Audio • Live-action Video VHS & DVD
is available in
French • German • Italian • Japanese • Spanish

LinguaFun!®
Language Learning Card Games with Audio
is available in
French • German • Italian • Spanish • Inglés

Learn in Your Car® for Kids™
Activity Book & Audio CD
is available in
French • German • Italian • Spanish

VocabuLearn® Beginners
Bilingual Language Learning with a Beat!
is available in
French • German • Italian • Spanish

Produced and distributed by
Penton Overseas, Inc.
The Global Language Specialists®

Call for FREE catalog
1-800-748-5804
www.pentonoverseas.com